Fact Finders®

Ar———————tion

Ancient Egyptian
Myths

By Kristine Carlson Asselin

Consultant:
Jennifer Houser Wegner, PhD
Associate Curator, Egyptian Section
Penn Museum, Pennsylvania

CAPSTONE PRESS
a capstone imprint

Fact Finder Books are published by Capstone Press,
1710 Roe Crest Drive, North Mankato, Minnesota 56003
www.capstonepub.com

Books published by Capstone Press are manufactured with paper
containing at least 10 percent post-consumer waste.

Library of Congress Cataloging-in-Publication Data
Asselin, Kristine Carlson.
Ancient Egyptian myths / by Kristine Carlson Asselin.
    p. cm. — (Fact finders)
Includes bibliographical references (p.   ) index.
ISBN 978-1-4296-7630-4 (library binding)
ISBN 978-1-4296-7977-0 (paperback)
1. Mythology, Egyptian—Juvenile literature. I. Title. II. Series.

BL2441.3.A54 2012
299'.3113—dc23

2011033954

Editorial Credits
Brenda Haugen, editor; Juliette Peters, series designer; Marcie Spence, media researcher;
    Laura Manthe, production specialist

Photo Credits
Art Resource, N.Y.: Erich Lessing, 11, 29, James Morris, cover; Bridgeman Art Library: Ancient Art
and Architecture Collection, 17, Brooklyn Museum of Art, New York, USA/Charles Edwin Wilbour
Fund, 23, Look and Learn, 24–25, The Stapleton Collection, 21; Corbis: Charles & Josette Lenars, 12,
Khaled Elfiqi/epa, 28; Getty Images, Inc.: Bob Thomas/Popperfoto, 14, DEA Picture Library/
De Agostini, 15, S. Vannini/De Agostini, 7, 26; Mary Evans Picture Library, 5, 19 (bottom);
Shutterstock: Julian de dios, 8, Steve Heap, 19 (top)

Printed in the United States of America in Brainerd, Minnesota.

102011   006406BANGS12

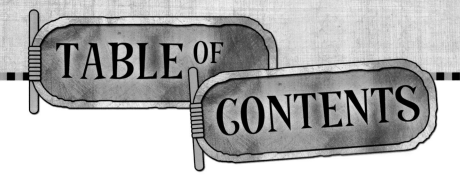

TABLE OF CONTENTS

The Myth of Osiris

When the world began, Egypt was in **chaos**. War and disorder were part of people's daily lives. Osiris became **pharaoh** and brought harmony to the people of Egypt. Osiris was a descendent of the god Ra. Ra was the creator of the world. People loved Osiris. He taught them to make bread and wine. He oversaw the construction of the first temples. He brought order to the world by making sure people knew the law and followed it.

But Osiris' brother Seth hated the pharaoh. He was jealous of how much the people loved Osiris. Seth wanted to be pharaoh.

One day Seth invited Osiris to a party in his honor. The party included a feast. At the end of the meal, Seth unveiled a beautifully decorated chest. He offered it as a gift to the person who could fit perfectly inside the chest. Like a party game, each guest tried to fit inside. Some guests were too big. Others were too small. Seth had made sure the chest was exactly Osiris' size and would not fit anyone else.

Osiris wedged himself into the chest. He fit perfectly and was awarded the beautiful gift. But he didn't get to enjoy the prize. Seth and his men slammed shut the lid of the chest and sealed Osiris inside. Then they threw the chest into the Nile River.

Orisis' wife, Isis, and Seth's wife, Nephthys, searched for the body of the murdered pharaoh. When they finally found him, the two women begged Ra to help them prepare the body for burial. Osiris could not come back to life, but he became king in the underworld—the king of the dead. Seth never realized his dream of becoming pharaoh. Osiris and Isis' son Horus battled his uncle Seth for 80 years to take the throne. In the end, Horus won.

The story of Seth and Osiris was just one of many myths told by ancient Egyptians. For Egyptians, myths explained the mysteries of their world.

Osiris (left) about to climb into the chest

chaos: total confusion; anything that throws the world out of balance, such as war

pharaoh: a king of ancient Egypt

5

Chapter 1

Ancient Egypt's Religion and Myths

Ancient Egyptians believed in a complex web of gods and goddesses. These beings helped Egyptians understand the world and their place in it. People held their gods and goddesses responsible for almost every part of life. Many of these gods took human form but just as many were animals. Some were a combination of human and animal, such as a male body and a falcon head. Others changed shapes, depending on their duties.

Ancient Egyptians based their religion on things they could see or touch. These things included animals, the sun, the moon, the river, and crops. They often told myths. These stories told of gods interacting with an ordinary part of the world. Through myths, people could explain terrible things such as droughts, **famines**, or the deaths of loved ones. Myths also explained wonderful things, such as the birth of a child or winning a battle. A big part of Egyptian religion centered on the ideas of chaos and order. Myths often explained why the world was sometimes thrown into chaos.

Many of the ancient Egyptian myths are known today through the remains of tombs and temples. Myths were painted on walls and carved in ancient **artifacts**. But many of the myths have been lost because buildings and artifacts were destroyed or buried.

famine: a serious shortage of food resulting in widespread hunger and death

artifact: an object used in the past that was made by people

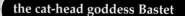
the cat-head goddess Bastet

7

the Nefertari temple

Religion in Daily Life

Ancient Egyptian daily life revolved around religion and myths. Religious rites accompanied births, marriages, parenthood, and death. Rituals often included using props, such as **amulets** worn around a person's neck or wands. Other rites included saying a spell at a certain time or tying a person's hair back in a tight knot. People also believed that gifts to certain gods or goddesses could solve problems and keep them healthy. If they were desperate, people traveled to a god's temple. There they would plead for something specific, such as a return to good health.

amulet: a small charm believed to protect the wearer from harm

Common people were not allowed to enter the temple. They could go to a courtyard near the entrance. Once the temple was complete, builders were only allowed inside for repair work. Only kings and priests entered the deepest sections of a temple.

Time to Celebrate

Many of the gods and goddesses had special festival days. Ancient Egyptians believed gods loved to hear singing, chanting, and music. A ritual statue was removed from the temple during a festival. A priest carried the statue during the celebration. But the statue was enclosed in a special container called a barque shrine. Priests carried the shrine on their shoulders. The statue of the god was considered sacred and normally stayed in the temple.

Chapter 2

Myths about the World

The ancient Egyptians used myths to describe the beginning of the world and other things they could not explain. Myths often used main characters to explain a complex situation or idea.

In one version of an ancient Egyptian creation myth, the sun god, Ra, made the world. He simply stepped out of the nameless sea and spoke his own name. Whatever Ra imagined he created. He sneezed and his children Shu (Air) and Tefnut (Rain) were born. Ra named the River Nile. And he called the land Egypt.

FACT

Ancient Egyptians worshipped more than 1,500 gods.

The children of Shu and Tefnut were Nut (Sky) and Geb (Earth). Nut and Geb were brother and sister but are often pictured as husband and wife. Nut and Geb had four children.

one version of the creation of the world

Egyptians harvesting their crops

In the ancient Egyptian religion, all life was descended from nine gods called the Ennead. The Ennead included Ra, Shu, Tefnut, Geb, Nut, Isis, Osiris, Nepthys, and Seth. Geb and Nut's children became Egypt's most important gods. These children were the enemy brothers, Osiris and Seth. Their sisters, Isis and Nephthys, are often described as the wives of Osiris and Seth.

The people who believed this story of creation lived near the Nile River. Every year the river flooded. When the water retreated, it left behind fertile land. Bountiful crops grew in this rich soil and fed the people. The myth of the sun god creating the earth as he stepped out of the water fits perfectly into this world.

The Ennead

The nine gods who make up the Ennead are the most important gods in ancient Egyptian religion.

Ra—god of the sun. Ra was the creator of the world and all the other gods.

Shu—god of the air, father of Geb and Nut, and brother and husband of Tefnut. Shu is often shown as holding the body of Nut above Geb.

Tefnut—goddess of moisture, mother of Nut and Geb, and sister/wife of Shu. Tefnut is often shown as a lioness.

Geb—god of earth, son of Shu and Tefnut, brother/husband of Nut, and father of Osiris. Geb was associated with the well-being of the earth and livestock.

Nut—goddess of the sky, daughter of Shu and Tefnut, and sister/wife of Geb. People believed Nut's laughter was thunder, and her tears were rain.

Osiris—god of death, rebirth, and fertility; son of Geb and Nut, and brother/huband of Isis. Osiris was believed to be Egypt's pharaoh until he was killed by his brother, Seth.

Isis—worshipped as a healer and magical goddess; daughter of Geb and Nut, sister/wife of Osiris, and mother of Horus. Ancient Egypt's most important goddess, Isis was often shown as the mother of all pharaohs.

Seth—god of violence, confusion, and chaos; son of Geb and Nut, brother of Osiris, and brother/husband of Nephthys. Seth killed Osiris to claim the throne of Egypt, but his nephew Horus would win the crown instead.

Nephthys—strongly associated with her sister, Isis; daughter of Geb and Nut and sister/wife of Seth. Nephthys often appears beside her sister as a supporter and helper of Osiris.

The Days of the Year

The myth of Nut's children explains the days of the year and the phases of the moon. The story was recorded by Greek historian Plutarch. It says that one day Ra became angry at Nut and cursed her. Because of the curse, Nut could never have children—not in any day of any year. In ancient times there were 360 days in a year. Nut's good friend Thoth felt sorry for her, so he challenged the moon to a card game. Each game he won, Thoth asked for a bit of moonlight. In time each piece of moonlight added up to five days—making the year 365 days. Each of Nut's children was born on one of these extra days, which were not included in the curse. The moon lost so much light in the card game that it had to conserve what remained. The moon could no longer shine full all the time.

FACT

In some cases, the stories told by Greek historian Plutarch are the only complete versions of the ancient Egyptian myths. Pieces of Egyptian text that have been found support his versions of the myths.

Plutarch

A scene from the creation story with the sky goddess Nut covered with stars

Order and Chaos

Ancient Egyptians believed their pharaohs were gods. They considered the pharaoh the **reincarnation** of Horus. Many myths centered around the pharaoh.

The king was often viewed as the human image of the god Horus, son of Osiris and Isis. Horus was the soaring falcon and the sky god, whose right eye was the sun and left eye the moon. He united Egypt after Seth brought chaos when he killed Horus' father, Osiris.

The ancient Egyptian people believed that the universe was made of order and chaos. The pharaoh's biggest responsibility was to maintain order and keep chaos away. Chaos always lurked just around the corner. But harmony could win as long as order existed.

Myths often reflected the struggle between order and chaos. One example of this fight is the story of Apophis and Ra. Apophis, a huge snake, existed at the beginning of time. He came out of the same dark waters that Ra had used to create the world. An enemy of Ra, the snake attacked the sun when it set each night. Every night the sun god fought and defeated Apophis. But since the snake was **immortal**, the fight never really ended. The real fear of snakebites and the uncertainty of everyday life are shown in stories like this. People feared a snakelike god who caused chaos.

Ra, in the form of a cat, slays Apophis.

reincarnation: the rebirth of a soul in a new body

immortal: able to live forever

Discovering Myths

Ancient Egyptian myths often include stories of gods and goddesses who talk, play, and fight with humans. The wind on your face might be the air god Shu walking by. An unusual smell might be the presence of a goddess. A demon or the ghost of a dead relative might be the cause of a headache. There was a god or goddess for almost every part of life and death.

Archaeologists believe that real events and real people might have inspired some myths. Many myths began before people started recording history and survived to the end of the ancient world. More myths have been lost because people didn't write them down or they were not saved. Scientists believe it is possible that more myths are waiting to be discovered.

FACT

Egyptian myths are like jigsaw puzzles. Sources are written in a variety of languages and script—such as hieroglyphs. To solve the puzzle, these languages must be unlocked.

archaeologist: a scientist who studies how people lived in the past

The Eye of Horus

Egyptian myths continue to influence modern people. In the Mediterranean, it is traditional for sailors to paint an eye on their boats for protection. Most don't realize this is a custom that goes back to the Eye of Horus.

Breaking the Code

Archaeologists have discovered paintings and artifacts telling the stories of the gods in temples and tombs. They have also found stories written on scrolls. For many years, decoding these stories was impossible. In 1799 French soldiers found an artifact called the Rosetta Stone. This discovery changed everything. The Rosetta Stone was carved in 196 BC and says the same thing in three ways. It's written in Egyptian hieroglyphs, an Egyptian language called Demotic, and Greek. When the Rosetta Stone was finally decoded in 1822, archaeologists could translate other ancient writings.

Chapter 3

Myths about Power

Many myths demonstrated knowledge and power. The most powerful goddess, Isis, was loved for protecting children. Before Seth killed her husband, Isis worked with Osiris to teach people how to farm. She gave them the secret of medicine and started the custom of marriage. She was so clever she tricked Ra.

After the death of Osiris, Isis wanted her son, Horus, to become king. To make sure of this, she planned to trick Ra into telling her his secret name. By chance she came upon Ra napping with a long stream of drool hanging from his mouth. Mixing a drop of the drool with a bit of clay, Isis formed a venomous snake. She released the snake in a place where it would bite Ra.

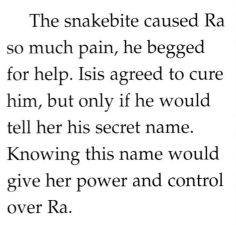

Isis and Ra

The snakebite caused Ra so much pain, he begged for help. Isis agreed to cure him, but only if he would tell her his secret name. Knowing this name would give her power and control over Ra.

He refused to tell her again and again. Finally he couldn't stand the pain any longer. He agreed to share his name, but Isis was to tell no one but Horus. Isis cured Ra, and he gave Horus the ability to defeat Seth and become king.

There are many myths and legends about Isis. Because of this myth, Isis was considered one of the most magical gods. Many ancient Egyptians worshipped her. When loved ones were sick, ancient Egyptians begged Isis to heal them.

The Destruction of Mankind

Isis was not the only goddess. Many myths centered on powerful women. Hathor, the cow goddess, protected mothers and children. In another form, she was Ra's eye. Ra sometimes sent Hathor on errands to punish his subjects. During these times, Hathor took the shape of a lioness.

When Ra became old, he feared the people would overthrow him. He wanted to show them he was still a powerful king. He sent Hathor in her lioness form to punish mankind. But she lost control of her power. By the time Ra called her back to him, Hathor was determined to wipe out all people. Ra did not want mankind destroyed. He only wanted to show people that he still had power.

Ra sent messengers to make a drink for Hathor that looked just like blood. They spread the liquid in the fields. Hathor drank so much that she fell asleep. When she woke, she forgot about destroying mankind and became a kind and gentle goddess once again.

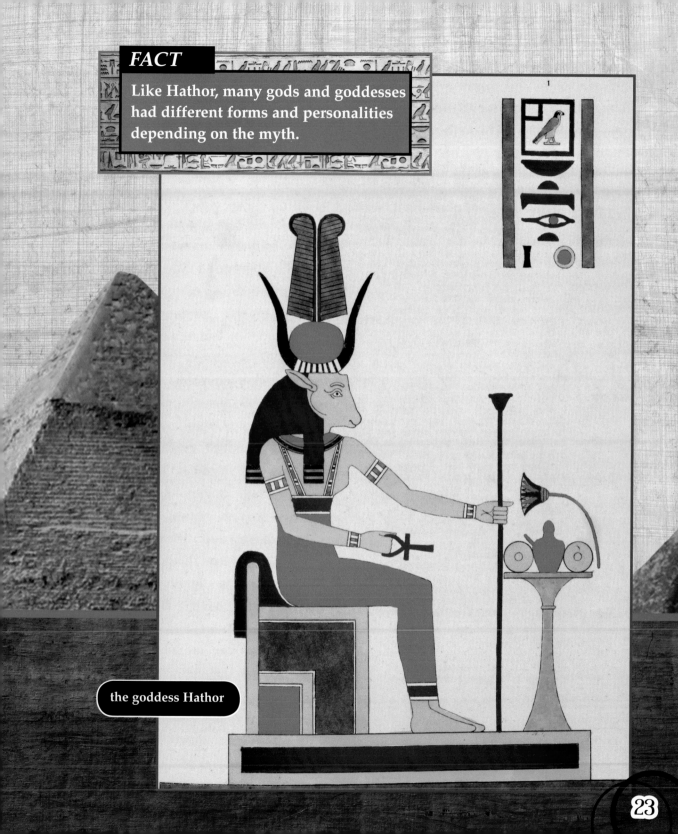

the goddess Hathor

Chapter 4

The Afterlife

Ancient Egyptians believed in the **afterlife**. They believed that death was not the end, but a new form of life. One of the first jobs a pharaoh had after he was crowned was to begin work on his own tomb. He had to prepare the resting place for his body after he died. The people considered their dead pharaohs to be on the same level as gods.

Pharaohs were also expected to build temples to the gods. If a king pleased the gods, he would join them in the afterlife. The average person would avoid a terrible place in the afterlife by leaving gifts at the gods' temples.

afterlife: the life that begins when a person dies

The pharaoh was not the only one related to gods. Ancient Egyptians believed that each object in the universe had a soul. Belief in magic and superstition was part of all ancient Egyptians' daily lives. Animals, in particular, had certain characteristics the people admired or feared. Some were beautiful. Some were strong. Some were fast.

A pharaoh watches a temple being built.

A soul is weighed in front of the baboon god Thoth.

Gods and goddesses often shared the qualities of animals. They sometimes took the forms of the animals with whom they were linked. For example, Horus is often pictured as a man with a falcon's head. Taweret, a minor goddess who helped mothers, was shown as a hippopotamus. Thoth, the god of wisdom, was linked with baboons and some birds. Bastet was worshipped as a cat. Ancient Egyptians honored cats above most other animals because cats could kill snakes.

The belief in a life after death was an important part of the ancient Egyptian religion. If people prepared properly for death, then life would continue in the afterlife. Pictures of everyday life as well as retellings of many myths appear on tomb walls. These images would always remind the dead of the way they lived. Bodies were buried with pots, jewelry, weapons, and other tools they might need. If they could afford it, Egyptians spent most of their lives—and resources— preparing for the afterlife. To help make it safely to the afterlife, people worshipped Osiris, King of the Dead.

FACT

Anyone who spent time on the Nile River had to deal with dangerous crocodiles. Various temples to the crocodile god, Sobek, were built to ward off the danger. Boaters also used spells, amulets, and hand gestures to protect themselves.

Chapter 5

Legacy of Egyptian Myths

Images of cows and falcons worshipped by ancient Egyptians have been found at archaeological digs. These images turned into rich and detailed stories of the gods and life in ancient Egypt.

When Rome conquered Egypt in 30 BC, the Romans took a liking to Egyptian art. Egyptian symbols even appeared on early Roman coins. By the time Christianity came to Egypt in the second century AD, the ancient religious traditions were fading. But Egyptians saw many of their own myths in the early Christian stories.

Egyptian culture made its mark on the country's friends and enemies. Even today, the influence of ancient Egyptian myths is found in movies, video games, and books. And archaeologists are still discovering more about these ancient stories and the way of life they represent.

GLOSSARY

afterlife (AF-tur-life)—the life that begins when a person dies

amulet (AM-yoo-let)—a small charm believed to protect the wearer from harm

archaeologist (ar-kee-AH-luh-jist)—a scientist who studies how people lived in the past

artifact (AR-tuh-fakt)—an object used in the past that was made by people

chaos (KAY-os)—total confusion; anything that throws the world out of balance, such as war

famine (FA-muhn)—a serious shortage of food resulting in widespread hunger and death

immortal (i-MOR-tuhl)—able to live forever

pharaoh (FAIR-oh)—a king of ancient Egypt

reincarnation (ree-in-kar-NAY-shuhn)—the rebirth of a soul in a new body

superstition (soo-pur-STI-shuhn)—a belief that an action can affect the outcome of a future event

READ MORE

Forest, Christopher. *Ancient Egyptian Gods and Goddesses.* Ancient Egyptian Civilization. Mankato, Minn.: Capstone Press, 2012.

Limke, Jeff. *Isis and Osiris: To the Ends of the Earth.* Graphic Myths and Legends. Minneapolis: Graphic Universe, 2007.

Shuter, Jane. *How the Ancient Egyptians Lived.* Life in Ancient Times. New York: Gareth Stevens, 2011.

Steele, Philip. *Ancient Egypt.* Passport to the Past. New York: Rosen Pub., 2009.

INTERNET SITES

FactHound offers a safe, fun way to find Internet sites related to this book. All of the sites on FactHound have been researched by our staff.

Here's all you do:

Visit *www.facthound.com*

Type in this code: 9781429676304

Super-cool stuff! Check out projects, games and lots more at **www.capstonekids.com**

INDEX